ALONG THE WAY

ALONG
THE WAY

poems for the wayward

C.M. RIVERS

WAYFARER BOOKS
BERKSHIRE MOUNTAINS, MASSACHUSETTS

All Rights Reserved
Published in 2023 by Wayfarer Books
Cover Design and Interior Design by Leslie M. Browning
Cover Image © Javier Allegue Barros
TRADE PAPERBACK 978-1-956368-46-8

10 9 8 7 6 5 4 3 2 1

Look for our titles in paperback, ebook, and audiobook wherever books are sold.
Wholesale offerings for retailers available through Ingram.

Wayfarer Books is committed to ecological stewardship.
We greatly value the natural environment and invest in conservation.
For each book purchased in our online store we plant one tree.

PO Box 1601, Northampton, MA 01061

860.574.5847 | info@homeboundpublications.com

HOMEBOUNDPUBLICATIONS.COM & WAYFARERBOOKS.ORG

For the teachers ~ so many

For the teachers ~ in other words,
anything we are willing to be a student of

For the teachers ~ who believe in us
before we know how to believe in ourselves

CONTENTS

PART TWO ~ SEEKING PASSAGE

PART THREE ~ HOMEBOUND

"Waywardness is a practice of possibility at a time when all roads, except the ones created by smashing out, are foreclosed. It obeys no rules and abides no authorities. It is unrepentant. It traffics in occult visions of other worlds and dreams of a different kind of life."

—SAIDIYA HARTMAN

PART ONE

~

REFUGEES
WELCOME

"...how way leads on to way..."
—ROBERT FROST

EAVESDROPPING ON LIFE

we thirst
to see clearly

unobstructed
but we're half-blind

we hunger to act
tirelessly

but we become tired
sometimes the rain

gets caught between
these two things

from a crack in the ground
flowers rise and shine

There are the crystals you left as blessings, tucked beneath the skin of the earth.

There is the love you have for everyone you feel separated from.

There are the invisible arrows that keep you on the path, so when some try to yoke you with doubt, saddle you with questions, you know well enough to tune your ear to a different frequency.

There is the learning that seems to come geologically slow, but eventually you remember to *forget them* (forget them!) and pay attention to the voice at your center, and through the acknowledgment of your voice you come to know your center, and you come to hold it.

There are the great jagged vertical stones, and also the small round ones.

There are the trees, connected— like us— in unseen ways by unseen roots. There is the road, your shoes, the bread, the wine, the good soup carried by kind hands.

There are all your prayers on display in the world around you, on the path before you. You don't need anyone's advice, you only need the ability to pay attention— that which you already possess, but do not always employ.

There are places to rest along the way of all your days, if you would only rest. There are ferries to bear you across every river, if you would only board them.

Sleep now. When you wake, it will still be here: this thirst to connect, this hunger to act, to move out-up-through-from-into.

Take your time, that's what it's there for. Walk to the ends of the earth.

Now, choose something to burn. What will it be?

CALIFORNIA

As morning reaches the coastal wetland
just off the beach, three egrets huddle
as if sketched into the lower left corner
of a Japanese woodblock painting,
each celestial neck folded in among itself,
ivory as an angel's raiment,
straight out of some ancient scroll, born
of brush-strokes presented with a flourish,
a flick of the village artist's wrist
at the old master's tea ceremony.

Wow, it's beautiful here even in January.

Shadows fold themselves up to pocket-size;
waves of solar gold hurl themselves against
the mountains, shameless, reckless.
The egrets begin to stir, and to my surprise
they are not egrets at all, but a homeless woman
who spent the night beneath a white sheet.

How much of life is conjecture;
how quickly is paradise lost
when truth executes a hit-and-run,
coaxing you into believing
the only honest gold left here
is indeed in the sunlight,
or perhaps the corroded fillings
in an old vagrant's mouth.

HIGH ROAD

Once you have traveled
      in the four directions,
along the main thoroughfare,
      and spent a good deal of time
on back roads and side roads,
      putting one foot in front
of the other until you reach
      a measure of satisfaction,
it is possible you might find
      a clear idea of why you set out
in the first place, so long ago.
      That's the high road—
from which you can look
      beyond yourself and see
how the course you take
      converges with all the others.
The cartography of your choices
      that seemed before to hold
no pattern— the direction of
      your footsteps, how
they brought you here at last.

UNIVERSITY

At half past seven   in the morning
you can sit   on cement steps
in a chilly stairwell   with closed eyes
hands on your knees   legs folded

a five-minute break   in uniform
chill wind meeting   your skin
your bones   greeting the cold
breathing

an old familiar song   air brakes at the bus stop
geese weathering overhead
a groundskeeper's lawnmower   starting up

EMERGENCE

My silent night, my holy night,
was not in December but in spring.
Nothing about my life had escaped
change.

How bizarre to be waiting
for sleep in the back of a car
in a tech-company parking lot,
Israel's first take on *Somewhere
Over the Rainbow*
pulling me into his bittersweet
longing, angel heard on high,
unexpected catalyst.

My body gave up
its long-held grief all at once,
a mother's arms relieved
of her baby, the wrenching
of a bottle from drunk hands.
The old self mourns
the death of itself,
a resurrected one
takes its place.

That's how it happens:
something in you opens
as something else closes,
leaving you on the doorstep
of decision,

as awkwardly alive as any
newly-hatched creature,
set adrift from day one
on a sea of circumstance.

ZEN

fingers of light
    touch the garden

green things grow thick
    'round the entranceway

spotted fawns have come by,
    mother not far behind

cat sits and watches

GOOD HANDS

Imagine
finding
yourself
in them.

Then
imagine
discovering
they've
been
yours
all along.

CERAMICS

You never know
when you might see
yourself.
Not a glance
in the mirror,
not a reflection
in the window.
See.

What you once
swore was solid
now reveals
its transparency:
you are translucent.
Temporary.
What once appeared
to be a stone
is exposed
as a feather.

The cup held
to your lips
slips from your hand,
breaks at your feet.
Not bothering to sweep,
you pack the car.
You pack
the car
and go.

You take everything
they thought
they knew about you,
every filament
of who they suspect
you are,
and you burn it.

Cradling ashes
in your palm,
you blow.

Window down,
music up,
foot leaning hard
into the accelerator.

NOTHING TO DECLARE

Seeping into   winter's marrow,
   the heartbeat   of the world
becomes available to me
in the formless clothing
of a silence so immense,
   I unravel, my passing made detectable.
The blown glass of pronouncement
     shatters, collapses in on itself.

  All of life is eating eating eating
   I will be food soon—
    I will be the nourishment
  required by other organisms.
I'll not see again   the body of spring;
    blood cell tissue bone muscle.
Yet spring will know   my body,
earth assimilate   my flesh,
  announce   its noiseless exhilaration
    in decomposition.

  Now come the voices
from outside   the tendrils   of time.
   Renounce honor, they murmur.
  Leave illusion, declaration.
  Forget scorn, forget measurement,
abandon   the posturing   of intellect.
Nothing left to name.
             Go in peace.

Valiant though it is to strive
for victory, the white fire of surrender
lights everything in its path
with greater   illumination.

BLUE SHUTTERS

When we press
our faces up against the glass
of what we suspect is possible,
then shall we find
ourselves tangled, intertwined,
sparks iridescent,
luminous strands coalescing.

Flint and tinder, we shift,
weave around potholes
on the way to the cape.
Understood or judged,
we care not.
The sand is coarse;
it clings to our oiled thighs,
the tops of our feet.
How long has it taken
to arrive here? Long.
Far beyond the travel-time.
Our lives mimic the dunes:
ever fragile, constantly reshaping,
held together by unseen roots.

Back on the mainland,
away from these pastel houses
with their blue and white shutters
and their decks peppered
with maritime bric-a-brac,

it will take greater effort to see
the most impermanent thing
in the world is us.

MOON SO BRIGHT

Many have already written this poem and hung it in their houses.
While crossing the river by ferry, some recite it, moon so bright.
Others burn it, or keep it in their pocket, or send it downstream.

The seasons of the body are well-known, moon so bright.
But what of the secret self?

Move into stillness, moon so bright. If possible,
lengthen the breath— if this is not possible, let it be less important.

Make a sound plan but expect it to change, moon so bright.
Look: the commonplace is rare; the ordinary, exquisite.
Whatever lies just outside your door is exotic to somebody, moon so bright.

Work willingly, work joyfully. If this seems impossible, begin to ask questions.
You are not here to define, categorize, or have expectations, moon so bright.

Sharpen the necessary tools, shed what is no longer useful, take inventory.
The mind is a secondary organ to the heart, moon so bright.

This planet is called Earth only because we label it as such.
We have draped the clothing of explanation over everything, moon so bright.
What if we loved all of it, no matter the cost?

A love so vast, exposed, serendipitous, revolutionary—
unbearable its confinement.

All day long, you see things a painter would paint. What is there to complain about? The road has been thoroughly mapped by the countless who have gone before you, revealed in sculpture, accounted for by poets, symbolized in myth, channeled in music and movement, meditated on by meditators.

Pilgrimage, healing, holding oneself in friendship— all these have relevance to your experience. Sing, minstrel, of the windswept mountainside, of the mud and the flood, of the light through the trees, starry blankets thrown over the world.

Search yourself. You will endure those who misunderstand, who expect and find their expectations unmet. You will suffer the tyranny of a mind that will do anything to maintain its governance.

To the world, you say *I'm sorry for so many things*. But to the world, you also say *thank you, thank you, thank you*.

SERVICE WORKER

We may not live to see the harvest,
gather the bounty, savor the meal,
or enjoy the kindly shade of the tree.

These may all very well
be the province of others.

So let us not forget our purpose,
overlook the importance of our labor,
neglect to take notice of our responsibility
or be blind to our blessings

in the patient growing of things,
the careful choosing of words,
the daily provision of nourishment.

May we observe
the wisdom of the camel,
who teaches well how to kneel,
how to work, carry water.

A HANDFUL OF DAYLIGHT

A tremor in the foundation,
the end of things as we know them.
We tend not to speak of rising water,
just quietly construct our levees.

Every day is reckoning day when we live like this.
Stripping the land of the things we need,
we sever the hand that holds our feed.

We might imagine ourselves
kindling a great bonfire,
pitching into it all our misgivings
until nothing remains
but smoke and cinders,
and we stand smudged with ash,
turning our faces up to a sky
now blue only in memory,
staring into what we have done,
left to wonder
what on Earth
we were thinking.

PREP

urgency and kindness
in his hands

toasting the rice
the old cook prances

almost struts,
outside a scrub jay

and nuthatch work
together, knocking

on a walnut branch
for grubs and such

MIRACLES

Sit, eat. Stand, walk.
Touch, see. Listen, talk.

Sleep, wake, again, wake.
Breathe, receive, give, take.

Gently, gently, go your way.

Heat hands with embers,
cool them with clay.

Bow, surrender, offer in kind.
Breathe, rise, shine.

ZOOLOGY

Tiger migrations:
sun, shade, sun, shade.
Ever-turned-away
from the watchers.
Looking out through tiger eyes,
thinking tiger thoughts.
Swish, the tail. Each swish
an affirmation of primal power,
regal grace.
Each muscular ripple, each twitch
a psychic message in a tiger bottle.
That others might come,
that they might leave, together,
this place of human curiosity.

The elephant understood.
Lucid, comprehending,
her heart stronger than mine.
She understood why I kept looking
away, failing to deny the ships
that break upon rocks every day.
Strange that she should find
acceptance more easily than I.

The lion spoke directly.
Why have you come?
I don't come
to watch you sleep,
to watch you pace
from room to room,
gazing through windows
with sad eyes,
cleaning meat from bones
given you.
Do what is denied of me:
go home.

SHELTER

Traces of calm, murmurs
    heard only in silence.
Not the stuff of dreams,
    but rest. Refuge.
She is fluent with herself
    in ways that are not language.
She sees herself,
    clear sight penetrating.
Her hand brushes across the wood
    floor upon which she lays.
Outside, evening gathers,
    harvests the light to sow itself.
Inside, she gathers her own self
    inside the first real sense of shelter
she's ever known— rooted, unshakable.

    Now, she begins to rise.
She notices, for the first time, this rising—
    it's quiet. It goes unnoticed by others.
She thinks of a prism,
    how it sheds light, fractures it.
Feeling like a crystal herself,
    she stretches, almost an animal.
It is the most exquisite stretch
    her body has ever tasted.
She drinks until there's no breath left,
    as if the moment were a still pool
from which all else rippled outward.
    She savors every molecule, every atom,
and splits a few new ones.

ARTS AND CRAFTS

A carpenter watches the point being sawed,
the seamstress trains her eye upon the needle.
The monk rests his awareness on the hinge
from which the door of breath opens and closes.

Only quality of mind changes as the artist
interprets the language of living a life,
the craftsman conversing with earthly conditions;
the viewer and the view.

Now comes a rush of cosmic wind:
the blink of an eye that is your life,
with its work and its weather,
rhythms and revelations.

It's sort of like knitting:
your life the thread, the world
a vast material, the needle of time
pulling you intricately through.

Or maybe the needle is life itself,
all ruinous sin and saintly ambition,
artistry and order, craftsmanship and chaos:
the Road up and over the Mountain.

It's sort of like weaving, but the hands
are invisible and not always kind.
It's sort of like watching a wheel go around:
this living, this loving, this mind.

CARPENTER

Nothing
centers you more
than squaring things
up.

Level-headed,
you straighten,
take the measurements
of creation.

Feel
along the rough
and the smooth
for the grain
of what truth is
to you.

PART TWO

~

SEEKING
PASSAGE

~

---

*"Show me your face before
your parents were born."*
ZEN KOAN

SEEKING PASSAGE

The skin around your knuckles is gathering, separating,
the lines of your palms deepening   into rifts, punctuating
   the landscape   of a mortal body.

         Everyone you've ever loved is leaving you.
Don't act so surprised.

     Your line grows heavy with each passing day;
you wade further out into the current... (No— you're being pulled.)

      Your life is breaking open,
         cool smooth sheets of moonlight drape
    themselves over you, carve

their memories on the cavern walls of who you are, notes left
         by someone who can answer all your questions:
    not some powerful mysterious shaman—
     you. The only thing you need

   to know about your Self

         is there isn't one.

     Life, how do I hold thee? Softly.
World, how do I walk with thee? Closely.

    You open up, electric as you can, stretch out
         broad as anything.

It's the same as joining your hands in front of your heart,
　　　　　folding prostrate on the ground, palms up.

It's easy now, letting go of everyone,
　　　when forgiveness makes enough room
　　　　　　inside for them.

While you live, the world is changing, changing
all around you.

　　　What other way
　　　　　would you have it?

LAYERS

Sometimes it comes up in geology
or seasonal clothing decisions
but where it really gets me
is when I'm mopping, dusting
wiping, scrubbing
taking out the garbage
or killing ants

attempting to rinse
myself of the inevitable
trying to beat back
all that will come regardless

what a losing battle
the way we yearn
to get free of rot
to add a shine, a freshness
to all that withers

how we bury the truth
in noise and activity
have a great day
we practically shriek it

how inexorable
the way it approaches
the unstoppable tools
it uses to get the job done

so quiet and certain
beneath the hustle and bustle
you can almost hear the clock
of the heart stop ticking
no room for argument

only the blur of things passing
too close to the window
at breakneck speed
cheek pressed hard against the glass
you feel a little sick
though you seem to be getting
where you need to go

TRANSMIGRATION

You gave up for a while,
left yourself lying on the ground
of a clearing, among wild creatures
who heard you cry out for safe passage.
Something in you awakened, decided for itself
to leave willful ignorance behind,
to smash out of the cocoon.
And death refused the invitation,
rescheduled you.

How the poor lost child in you had changed
when you returned. How it welcomed you back,
and smiling easily, forgave you. And you,
ground down to a shaving by the wasteland,
were so ready to be freely held—
a wandering hound, lost and found, set gently
down on the doorstep by kind hands
that turned out to be your very own.

You befriended yourself, learned to live
again, and better, out in the storm
on the open sea that is so much more
the truth of who you are
than the safety of the harbor.

When we are busy living well and true,
death comes unasked for, comes to remind us
it owns the mortal house where we shelter,
the one we are convinced we own.

May we acknowledge what came before,
what is now, what may come.
Choose something to burn, toss the world away,
and in tossing it away hold it closer,
serve it better, be relentless
when it comes to reverence.

ANCHOR

When things unravel with such fury,
you conclude Something must be held responsible.

A master fly-fisherman of blame, you cast out—
though the Something is just things as they are,
disguised as the fear you hold tight to.
Or the Something might be the crown jewel
of all your denied cravings.

Either way, you hadn't expected lonesomeness
to be so vast. You didn't know
it would reach right into you
with its prairie-wind hands,
even when you're with someone you love.

A nameless urge tugs at your navel.
Sometimes you follow it head-first,
fevered with lust, careening
into wonderland.
Sometimes you turn instead,
both hands steady on your heart,
and look inside,
the way winter taught you.

SATORI

The boy lay in bed on his side
with his knees drawn up toward his chest.
A pillow was bunched up
beneath one side of his face,
one arm bolstering the pillow from beneath.
The other arm lay draped across his legs.
The long toes of his feet made
small movements while he dreamed
the dreams of one who is sleeping.
But sometimes he had other dreams—
the dreams of one who stays a short while
between sleeping and waking
on a feverish afternoon.
His most constant waking dream
was of taming the jaguar that roamed
near the house each evening at dusk.
The jaguar was dangerous
as the future, impulsive yet calculating,
and the boy knew then
that in order to tame it
he would have to tame himself.
He would have to stop eating
second and third helpings, stop lusting
after the merchant's daughter,
stealing from the marketplace.
Palm trees bent their heads down
like giraffes in the summer wind,
as if to remind him:
now that he knew this,
he could not un-know it.

Miracles, like thieves waiting to astonish an unwary tourist around the corner.

The appearance of ants, days ahead of rain. Burro dung holding up adobe walls for centuries. A hummingbird's heartbeat of over a thousand beats per minute. A blue whale's tongue weighing as much as an elephant. Humans owing their survival to all species of pollinators. The chance gift of the sun's proximity to this planet. Trees working tirelessly while appearing impossibly still. Heliotropism.

The slant of the light at a particular moment. Steam rising from a bowl of soup. A certain smell unleashing a cascade of memories in your brain: it could be cigar smoke, the leather interior of a car, the pages of a book, old-fashioned buttermilk doughnuts. A song opening a door inside you. Behind that door, a chapter of your life, a whole book, a series.

Naturally all this astonishment exhausts you, but it's a healthy exhaustion, like after a long day of hard work, body-surfing ocean waves, splitting firewood. The language of being alive inhabits you completely.

You come home to a bag of ripe plums a friend left at your door. Eating one, you celebrate its wine-red flesh. One day you'll be food for worms— maybe tomorrow— but for now you are here. You read a while. You extinguish the light, gently close your eyes down.

It's strange, you think, how there's no money in poetry, or bending spoons. And you're gone.

THE TURNING AWAY

Even those who were closest to you, even they—
once you could no longer be who they needed—
turned away. Things were different for them now,
as they were for you. Everyone stops at a viewpoint
eventually, looking over the landscape in all directions,
wondering what lies beyond the perceptible borders.

Some are never the same again,
but naturally they move on,
pushing through moments, days and nights
that turn, as if by enchantment,
into the broader measurements of time
that seem to contain them.

You move along too, uncertain
if you're falling up, down or sideways, or some new angle
that remains undiscovered, only dreamt about by astronauts.
Only now— having stopped at the vista point—
you decide not to push your way
through the moments anymore.
You lay back into them instead,
the way one lays in a hammock near the equator.

You see it more clearly now: how you tend to fall,
over and over, again and again.
You remember when your grandfather said
you have to know how to fall.

You notice how you do your own turning away,
how you make things up to stay busy,
how you're always striving to improve,
how you avoid at all costs
the possibility of being free
of the second-hand smoke
of all your sentimentality.

BEYOND THE FIELDSTONE WALL

You tilt on your axis.
    The other side of the canyon
seems impossible to reach.
    Give up the reaching
to find you contain the entire canyon,
    both sides, the floor, the entrance.
First this, then that.
    Stop clinging to any shred of proof
that you might be worth something.
    Trust, the way you trusted you wouldn't fall
that time you climbed the tallest tree
    beyond the fieldstone wall.

That moment was a specific point,
    a marker, a center known and held
in the infinite space of possibility.
    The air so soft, the tree so kind,
the glowing hemisphere of light so ethereal,
    you consumed that moment
and that moment consumed all of you.
    You fell in love with everything for the first time,
even the veins in your own hands, arms.
    Yet passing is what moments are made to do,
and this was no exception.

CANYON

You thought of how it was down there
in the in-between-ness,
the ears and eyes of the earth
rising up on either side of you.
The two walls have stood like that for eons, and still
they are always changing.
But on that particular night
they seemed to be rising up
in relation to you. Your body and the earth's body
are the same thing,
your flesh will one day become grass on a hillside,
become rain, mud, an apple.
You couldn't tell if the canyon was a cradle or a tomb,
so you decided it must be both.
(It would take six Earths to cover the distance
of Saturn's rings.)
Everything we do, we do on the primordial powder
of someone else's bones,
but you were never disenchanted with life,
even when your hair fell out and the wrinkles arrived
unfashionably early, and the back of your neck
gathered itself into a snowbank of blubber, and the callouses
on your feet became something reptilian,
still the silk scarf of enthusiasm burst from you.
Vibration accepted your invitation;
you made yourself a transmitter, a bringer, a carrier,
a tracker, a river winding along the canyon floor.

SAILING AND HOUSEKEEPING

Let me make my body a ship,
my heart its captain,
my attention first mate.
My spirit a compass,
a nautical star chart,
compassion the water
I navigate.

Let me make my body a house,
my intention a broom,
my mind the geometric beams.
My love, the foundation
that remains
of virtue, vice
and dreams.

CARTOGRAPHY

You go to the kitchen,
the garden, the forest,
the cave, the temple.

You make yourself small,
leaving signs.

That's how it's done:
you make yourself small
when you travel to another place.

Then you make your way back,
and find you are not the same person.

TURNING POINT

In the book
of my life
there is a chapter
and in that chapter
there is a page
and on that page
there is a paragraph
and in that paragraph
there is a line
in which I offer
love to myself
for the first time
since the beginning
of the book

INVITATION

Someday you will need to unravel
             the thread of hurt from the spool
  of your body.
                The invitation is to begin now.

        Light the first of many torches.
      Keep burning them until
          the way to healing opens,
   until the arena is so bright all your gladiators
cast down their swords
          and, blinded, kneel.

A MEASURE OF GRACE

When you empty the wheelbarrow
of rain-wetted weeds in the spring,
when the seashells along the garden wall
inspire you to sing,
think then, old friend, of how we once were,
and how years have fallen at our feet.

When the world is emptied of me and of you,
and our lifetimes dry up from their mornings of dew,
with the breath of the sun on the shimmering leaves,
remember then to say your prayers.

While the cat has a nap by the rocking porch-swing
and I've emptied the 'barrow of earth in the spring,
I'll think of you, fair weather friend,
and how there's a measure of grace about you.

By day, a daydream ponderer who never gets her fill;
by night a barefoot wanderer who's wandering still.
With my bones, crows, rocks and rain,
what a lucky so-and-so I shall be.

OREGON

the wood-heated house
>   of my remembered boyhood
smells of lentil soup

ELEVENTH BIRTHDAY

late August moon above the power plant
along the Columbia, Astoria to Portland
singing with mom in the old Audi Fox

PASSENGER

Here, it comes to me: am I still not free to go?
A memory of the future— this mother, this daughter,
this man, this animal. What is it like to be them?
What is it, inside them, that wishes for expression?
A memory of what is to come:
this is where the anger is kept, and also love.

The fog, how it lifts and settles again— the rain,
how it illuminates with long wet shadows.
This is the reversal of abandonment, the keeping
of the sacred fire, the sleeping assembly of facts,
structures of power inventing history.

What a mess you are sometimes beneath, though
on the surface no ripples— other times the inverse
of this, a point of stillness held in the eye,
the surface catastrophe, your life a chipped cup,
empty one day, overflowing another.

Passenger seeks refuge, refugee seeks passage.
It may be that our only obstacle is what we have become.

WHALE

and from you
I learned
how to go in deep

how to move
beneath
and sing

when the storm
breaks on the surface
wildly

WISH

I wish I knew what I used to know,
    but I had to get older, I had to grow;
if I remained a child and never grew,
    then now I'd know what I once knew.

PART THREE

HOMEBOUND

———

"Life is a short pause
between two mysteries."
—CARL JUNG

PILEATED WOODPECKER, EARLY APRIL

He prances.
Snow still clings
to the elbows of branches
as sapsucker's cousin
throws a glance.

Well-trained in his craft,
he is listening, listening
for what he inherently knows
about this particular tree:
there are provisions therein,
and thanks to evolution
he couldn't be better suited
for the task of acquiring them.

He seeks the essential,
what is necessary
to sustain life,
what he knows to be
the inflexible schedule
of survival.

Maybe that is why he works
the way he works: assertive,
and with such verve.
Perhaps he is strutting
his hard-won recognition
that things are what they are,
and nothing more.

MEETING GRAVITY

There's a buoyancy to the way one's bones surrender to the support of the ground, floor, earth. As if floating in salt water, there is a lightness held in the hand of heaviness.

Whether home, adrift, or in the sanctuary of yourself, once gravity meets you, you return to your center, withdraw from the limbs to anchor in the trunk, and your actions take root there.

The microcosm of the illusion of Self dances with the macrocosm of the Great Mystery. You locate yourself as if by compass, as if by magnetic force. Which way is in? Find out.

How gently, how merrily might you row down the stream, if only you allowed yourself to wander.

MERLYN

The mountains are alive with fire,
transcendent breath, vigorous and endless.
Though they have been given a name,
a part of them will always be nameless,
and I could say the same about myself.
I heed the call of mist-laden glades
and walk among stones with broken blades.
I come to you, mountains of fire,
full of so many things that matter,
yet they will not matter to you.
I come to you as a whittler of small days,
a worshiper of whale bones.
I come to you as a man who has a boy still looking
out from behind the bars of his rib cage.
I come to you with an owl on my shoulder
who comes and goes as she pleases.
I come to you as a failed magician,
with iron, ash, light, dust, rain
behind the cellar-door of knowledge.
I come to you as a broken lover,
a woman's hair still caught on my sleeves.
I come to you with the meaning of my name,
do with it what you will.
I come to you as the recorder
of my own life, pockets filled
with scribbled notes
of little use.

CONTINENTAL DIVIDE

The years groaned, turned over, shaking
the folds of the hours. Not fire, not flood,
but quietly, gradually.

Just as circumstance once pried us apart
into separate beds, separate rooms -
now decision rode out onto the field
with its own divisions.

Even in the space between two stages of molting
a whole life might be lived.

Only the language of time helps us to understand.
Our division struck the world, quivered
the aching arrow of it, yet the world took
no notice— it has seen much worse
than the two once entwined who are now no more.

Love did not abandon us; it stayed, held its course
until it shifted course. Changed and changed again.
I drifted, called away by other voices,
your voice behind me, distant, calling out my name.

A happy sound, for I know and love your voice
and because I need to be needed.
A sad sound, for I needed you
not to need me anymore.

ALCHEMY IN AUGUST

Forgive me for being so plain, but all things aside— including the steady stream of each moment pouring into the next— my purpose for being here today is to dive into the water, as far as I can tell. Viewed from above, this lake takes the shape of a long and crooked finger. Or you can go higher, to where the atmosphere brushes up against space, to see that finger as a fleshless bone. But from within, submerged in warm and cool pockets, the lake is velvet, polished, placid, for the moment undisturbed. It exists in a moment of perfect silence sought by many, discovered by few. It says:
"May my breath be your breath. My heat, yours. My fluid nature, yours. May you give up your crowded loneliness to me."
The lake's words ring true, as always. Sometimes we forget that we too are a part of nature— we, too, are included in the very thing that so often astounds us.

Hills, how they roll. Soft jewels laid to rest in summer's crown, with its high corn and its sunflowers drooping their heavy heads in holy silence.

Earth, how it turns. How it appears to be suspended in stillness beneath the touch of the sun, as if some unknown form of light has just this very moment been born and is shedding itself over the garden gate.

Mind, how it flickers. Static with the commotion of ten-thousand things. Thoughts whirling like dust rising in the wake of a galloping centaur, a storm bending evergreen boughs.

Rain: how it opens its mouth to speak. What have you lost sight of? Remember the three runes: Journey, Gateway, Awareness.

Evening: how it settles. How it applauds the dancer of the day, the cool cloth of its kindness coming to rest against the effortlessness of your spent body. And you try, all the while, for a little gratitude, a little grace.

STARLIGHT STAY

Starlight let me open to you, to the space between us. Please don't go to bed early. Stay up with me. Stay up late and let me not wither. Let mystery not be ponderous, but held lightly and without the use of my hands.

Stay into the deep hours when my mind's viscous broth comes to a rapid boil and my heart burns at a high and reckless temperature. Watch the fire through the window of my chest, smoke rising through the bars of my rib cage. Stay up with intricate whispers, elaborate cravings, convoluted borders, foreign languages, genie-like earlobes drooping.

Stand on the edge of the knife dividing sleep from awake, marvel at how alone and not-alone we all are, how the spirit voices are always there but do not just obediently come when called, how the tide is the sound of the ocean breathing.

And only once the marveling is done—only once I have been properly astounded, sufficiently rattled—let me surrender to the unremembered temple of well-fed lions—the drawn cloak of sleep.

DREAM CATCHER

Entering the West again. Returning into Vastness. Moving into
Stillness.

A dream of desire stirring below the navel. A dream of crouch-
ing at water's edge, sound of the bullroarer, coyote crossing my
path, turning, looking back, he this night twitching as he dreams
of the human who crossed his path.

The language of rivers, the accent of mountains, the ancient
dialect of trees, the lumbering grace of knowledgeable bears, the
leaping of salmon.

And then, the inevitable return, for after the dream I enter
myself again.

AN INCOMPREHENSIBLE FIRE

For many long years, sleep did not come.
Now it is here, a sanctuary,
a garden of bliss.

You slept: peaceful, grateful.
To start over, to unwrap the gift of a new beginning—
this is the chime of my intention for you.

Summer comes, undeniable as the desires of the body.
We peel away her clothes.
When she goes, we cannot go with her.

There will still be times we do not feel supported—
our connection to ourselves will always need
reestablishing.

There will still be times when pain holds us in its mouth
like a whale, and we struggle to light the way,
to see better in the dark.

The sun is rising again. The earth tilts on its axis
and that star is still there, incomprehensible fire of fires
at its center, moving ever outward,

cooling equally, creating a roundness.
We owe our life to the proximity of the earth
to the sun, to the distance between them.

We owe it to the motor in the ribcage,
to the lungs, working every moment in service to us.
It is morning and you are held in sleep.

I am held in my usual early wakefulness.
It is the end of my ego as it knows itself;
a newborn witness now.

Openness has cooled my burning.
The fastened container of my body aches
as I eat the world, and am eaten by the world.

WE CANNOT WAIT

We cannot wait for things to be different,
for things to be perfect, for things to meet
what we think we require.

We cannot wait for everyone's approval.
We cannot wait for the certainty
that everyone will agree
with what we have to say.

We cannot wait for ourselves to feel
less afraid.

We cannot wait for the road
to be clear before we cross it.

We have to step out into the danger.
We have to take the risk, loosen our grip
on everything we think we know.

We will be criticized, misunderstood:
still, we cannot wait.

That moment when all the world is before you, vast, undiscovered. When nothing about you has been decided, identified, known, by you or anyone. When you tear through the atmosphere, uncontainable, an afterburner of possibility. When you may as well have discovered fire.

That moment when you come up over the horizon, riding the edge between the realms of form and formlessness. The energy of your cells churning, streaking— individually, collectively— meteors across open space where a map of identity once hung on for dear life, on a journey toward decomposition, to be restructured by resurrection, transformed by incineration, alchemized by intention.

The high adventure of a simple, quiet life. Civilization, a blip on the radar. Humanity's rise and fall. External conditions. What is true? What might be a worthy use of your energy?

A HOUSE ALONG THE WAY

A spacious house is entirely unnecessary:
only let it contain kindness,
and each object within hold some purpose.

Let there be creaky floorboards in the hall,
a good sturdy soup pot, a sound kettle,
strong light for reading,
a good place for making love.
Let there be berries within an hour's walk.

Let me be a cabin, shack or shanty,
let me be a house along the seashore,
may I be a house along the way.

A rickety old wooden fence
crouching low to the sand,
a neighborly fox
sniffing at moonstones.

Let the morning symphony be
of whippoorwill, of seabirds,
the rustling of wind.
Let the light and heat of the afternoon
charge me, as if I were capable
of photosynthesis.

Should I become a vagabond
who sleeps in cars,
may it be near the sea
beneath shoreline stars.

A lakeshore will not do, nor a riverbank:
these cannot gather themselves up
and lunge at me as the sea does.

May we take to the sea,
give to it our grief;
may the ocean receive it,
the earth absorb it.

Let us leave stone and shell,
wind and wave,
for our fellow travelers to contemplate.
Let us not stay too long at sea,
lest we mistake a mirage for land.

We pray now to the buckwheat on the bluffs,
fall on our knees among the sage and yarrow.
Sleeping beneath knotted oaks, we untangle.
Kneeling among fallen acorns, we rise.

GHOSTS

One tries to lose them,
shake them off, but—
funny thing about ghosts—
they hang around.

The only trick that works,
works because it's not a trick,
not magic in the slightest:

to acknowledge what is true for you,
to make peace in the mind.
To dare, to turn, and look, and find
they are not ghosts at all,
but feelings you've been running
from, all your life.

Now, you ask yourself
to attend to what you have left
unattended.
To let yourself be seen and heard.

A tortoise summoning the courage
to flip onto its back,
a talker emerging
from the shelter of words.

TECHNIQUE

each place I go
> more astonishing than the last
> > (including nowhere)

this isn't a boast
> or foolishness
> > or any brand of luck

it's a way of seeing
> that has nothing to do
> > with eyes

PARABOLA

Across the vale, through the veil
you see yourself in the old man
across the river, who sees in you
himself reflected.

You walk many paths,
strike up a conversation
with the world,
hear the song of earth
in the cosmic auditorium.

The thunder of your life
crackles, yet time has an arc
and its archway lightens you.
You need lightening
because: gravity.

At Montana de Oro,
where the flat ocean plane
meets the base of the small peak,
you explore the wonders
existing in the arc between the two,
and so much gladdens you here:
a gray fox looking up from her breakfast.
A great slope of scorched manzanitas
peppered with wildflowers.
Turkey vultures hovering,
the phantom morning moon,
the bubbling creek, trilliums, gypsum,

seaside bluffs, scrub brush—
all the day's decorations.

And you find it again—
the earth's power to heal
pain, any pain,
so long as you are willing
to call it forth.

CARDINAL

While admiring eastern pines
this morning, I paused
to marvel at my heart
for knowing how to beat,

and also at the red bird
dashing briskly
along branches of holly,
eager to claim the berries
of color and liveliness
equal to his own.

He had a tiny snowcap
atop his head, and behaved
like such a gentleman
that I sensed less betrayal
in the world, and in myself
a trifle of harmony.

As a moment spent singing,
the sighting exalted me,
bringing me tidings
of gladness, as if he were
a winged incarnation
of Saint Nicholas himself.

SIGNS OF LIFE

The ice is melting, the eaves drip,
we're tipping back towards the sun.
Bursting like an outlaw from the edge
of the woodshed, a mouse
vanishes back through his hidden portal,
a flash of chestnut, an anomaly
after so many weeks of soundless, lifeless cold.
I imagine him returning to sleeping bag,
lighted lamp, a stack of books,
dreams of spring.

An almost indistinguishable pitter-patter
of yet another mouse nibbling at a cookie
left exposed on the blue-and-white tiles
of the kitchen counter.
Hoof-prints at the back of the house this morning,
on a furrowed path that runs through a shrunken canyon
between waist-high banks of snow.
March is underway. Everything eases up slightly.
Things have been draped down over themselves,
now they have their hands on their knees
and are beginning to rise.

Groundhog prepares her tea, rests in her chair,
thinks of the old fox who lived there before she moved in.
Wonders how he's doing these days. She always liked him.

She had imagined, many times,
the two of them slow-dancing, burning a candle
at three in the morning,
her head against his fiery chest.

Back above ground, we long
to see beneath the snow.
We long for the northern door's latch
to unhook.

Back above ground, there go
the black-capped chickadees.
Birds who— like us—
have been around all winter.

FELLOW TRAVELERS

There is more than one world. Turn your attention now,
away from the one that is always trying to sell you something,
for time is short and you have work to do.

Befriend yourself, settle into a homecoming,
apprentice yourself to the dear friend of your own curiosity,
to a sense of belonging, a familiarity not dependent
on external circumstance, not interested in outward manifestation.
Do not overlook the possibility of something more radical.

Flash a smile and a sparkling eye
at every stranger you meet upon the road.
Your heart's voice will become so nourishing
resisting the call to drink from it shall be impossible,
easing your thirst with refreshment from your own well,
with plenty to spare for all fellow travelers.

Work all the morning alongside your comrades,
companions from every country, prophets from every land.
Walk all the afternoon among hills that rise and fall.
Rest all the evening, recite a verse three times
for health and good fortune.
Wake next morning, take a vow of kindness,
begin again.

ANOTHER COUNTRY

On the jade plate—
    a golden pear.

Between window and altar—
    bed on the floor.

In the shade of the forest—
    sound of water.

From a kettle in the kitchen—
    steam rising.

In a wrought-iron stove—
    embers glowing.

At the edge of autumn—
    all that I am.

HOMEBOUND

As a boy I walked along train tracks
munching sour-grass and clover.
I could feel the world breathing
up through my feet, into the rest of me,
and up through the bike wheels
as I rode along fields, orchards,
the edges of roads, woods and waters,
skirting the borders and boundaries
of an already half-forgotten innocence
sewn by the passage of years, making way
for an approaching horizon.

I knew not the meaning of haste,
darkness, powerlessness, responsibility.
I only knew that my mother and I sang
together while she drove the old car
upriver to the swimming hole,
or to see the Christmas lights strung
over the houses of city neighborhoods.
I only knew that I loved fried fish and remoulade,
the smell of book pages when I turned them,
the crackle of an old record,
the plunk of rain against a coffee can,
wood popping in the cast-iron stove. Quiet.
I heard the world whispering,
an inexorable summons calling
through the overgrown garden
of my childish imagination.

Of how time changes everything, I knew nothing.
Of wounding and of mending, I knew nothing.
Of how we might become lost
and how we might find our way again.
Of how we might come home to ourselves,
welcome and befriend ourselves.
Of how every breath can be a turn
of the wheel, setting a homeward course.

We are wayward on the horizon,
in the distance and the invitation.
In our departure, exile and return,
we are homebound in all directions.

WILDERNESS

Here, it comes to me.
A life's work—

no embrace, no rejection,
to neither cling nor condemn.

ACKNOWLEDGMENTS

My gratitude to the editors of the publications in which the following poems have previously appeared. Some poems may have since taken a slightly different form.

"Moon So Bright"; "Service Worker"; "Pileated Woodpecker, Early April"— *The Wayfarer*

"Zen"; "A Measure of Grace"— *Poetry Pacific*

"Starlight Stay"— *The Adirondack Review*

"Anchor"— *Two Hawks Quarterly*

"Wish"— *Soundings Review*

"Oregon"— *50 Haiku*

"Arts and Crafts" — *Gyroscope Review*

ABOUT THE AUTHOR

Also the author of *How To Carry Soup*, C.M. Rivers grew up reading to the sound of rain on the roof in Oregon. His poems have appeared in literary magazines across the United States. Discover more of his work at cmrivers.com, or on his podcast *Why Am I Telling You This?*

HOMEBOUND
PUBLICATIONS

Since 2011 We are an award-winning independent publisher striving to ensure that the mainstream is not the only stream. More than a company, we are a community of writers and readers exploring the larger questions we face as a global village. It is our intention to preserve contemplative storytelling. We publish full-length introspective works of creative non-fiction, literary fiction, and poetry.

Look for Our Imprints Little Bound Books, Owl House Books, *The Wayfarer Magazine,* Wayfarer Books & Navigator Graphics

WWW.HOMEBOUNDPUBLICATIONS.COM

WAYFARER

BASED IN THE BERKSHIRE MOUNTAINS, MASS.

The Wayfarer Magazine. Since 2012, *The Wayfarer* has been offering literature, interviews, and art with the intention to inspires our readers, enrich their lives, and highlight the power for agency and change-making that each individual holds. By our definition, a wayfarer is one whose inner-compass is ever-oriented to truth, wisdom, healing, and beauty in their own wandering. *The Wayfarer's* mission as a publication is to foster a community of contemplative voices and provide readers with resources and perspectives that support them in their own journey.

Wayfarer Books is our newest imprint! After nearly 10 years in print, *The Wayfarer Magazine* is branching out from our magazine to become a full-fledged publishing house offering full-length works of eco-literature!

Wayfarer Farm & Retreat is our latest endeavor, springing up the Berkshire Mountains of Massachusetts. Set to open to the public in 2025, the 15-acre retreat will offer workshops, farm-to-table dinners, off-grid retreat cabins, and artist residencies.

WWW.WAYFARERBOOKS.ORG

www.ingramcontent.com/pod-product-compliance
Lightning Source LLC
Chambersburg PA
CBHW031435120626
46545CB00006B/2412

* 9 7 8 1 9 5 6 3 6 8 4 6 8 *